Heart-to-Heart
with Women
Devotional

HEART-TO-HEART WITH WOMEN DEVOTIONAL

Practical Wisdom for Daily Living

Marcia K. Moragne-Wells

ELM HILL

A Division of
HarperCollins Christian Publishing

www.elmhillbooks.com

© 2020 Marcia K. Moragne-Wells

Heart-to-Heart with Women Devotional
Practical Wisdom for Daily Living

Published in Nashville, Tennessee, by Elm Hill, an imprint of Thomas Nelson. Elm Hill and Thomas Nelson are registered trademarks of HarperCollins Christian Publishing, Inc.

Elm Hill titles may be purchased in bulk for educational, business, fund-raising, or sales promotional use. For information, please e-mail SpecialMarkets@ ThomasNelson.com.

Scripture quotations marked KJV are from the King James Version. Public domain.

Scripture quotations marked NLT are from the Holy Bible, New Living Translation. © 1996, 2004, 2007, 2013, 2015 by Tyndale House Foundation. Used by permission of Tyndale House Publishers, Inc., Carol Stream, Illinois 60188. All rights reserved.

Scripture quotations marked NIV are from the Holy Bible, New International Version®, NIV®. Copyright © 1973, 1978, 1984, 2011 by Biblica, Inc.® Used by permission of Zondervan. All rights reserved worldwide. www.Zondervan.com. The "NIV" and "New International Version" are trademarks registered in the United States Patent and Trademark Office by Biblica, Inc.®

Scripture quotations marked NKJV are from the New King James Version®. © 1982 by Thomas Nelson. Used by permission. All rights reserved.

Library of Congress Cataloging-in-Publication Data

Library of Congress Control Number: 2020903991

ISBN 978-1-400331871 (Paperback)
ISBN 978-1-400331888 (eBook)

Acknowledgements

To my parents Louise & Felder Moragne
Thank you for your unconditional love and godly example. I have
become the woman I am because of your love and encouragement.

To the love of my life, my husband, William G. Wells
Thank you for your unconditional love and support.

To my children,
Tina, Adrianne, Erica, Marcus, Lisa, and William
Thank you for being my inspiration.

To the leading ladies and mentors in my life,
Sarah Rose Lewis, Margaret B. Moses,
Delinda Pendleton & Lesa Grant
Thank you for your example of the life of a godly woman.

INTRODUCTION

One day I asked myself this question "What have I done with my life." Have you ever been there? Life is a journey and sometimes we get so busy "doing life" that we do not take time to enjoy the journey or the rewards along the way. We tend to think more about what has gone wrong than to be grateful for what is going well. I have had many wonderful people mentor and encourage me and share things they thought I may do with my life and writing a devotional for women was not on the list. But here I am sharing my journey with you. The highs and lows, the victories, and what felt like defeat at the time have all worked together for my good.

I was blessed with parents with whom I could share my dreams and visions. My father was very encouraging and always told us to do whatever we chose to do in excellence. Mom was an extraordinary woman—the wife of a pastor and mother of fourteen children. She never complained about her role in our family and never once made us feel like a burden. She was an example to me and my five sisters of a godly woman and a homemaker. Our home was a well-kept haven. A place of love and joy. There were also times that called for discipline and my parents were definitely a team when those times came.

No playing one against the other in our home. But in all seriousness, it is because of my mother that I wanted to be the best wife and mother I could be.

We all know life brings joy and sorrow, ups and downs. I know it is not always easy and sometimes you cannot see your way. As women, we carry so much weight and at times life is like a juggling act. There are times when circumstances beyond our control cause hardships that may not seem fair. Sometimes you are doing all you know to do and still seem to get nowhere. There were so many beautiful godly examples for me, but I still had my own journey and had to trust God for myself. Even with all that was invested in me, it was up to me to apply what I learned.

Today, most women must work inside and outside of the home. My mother was a wife and mother who did not work outside the home. I had the pleasure of experiencing both staying at home for a time and having a career when the children were older. Mom and I often discussed the differences between women of her generation and mine. Expectations from men and society, in general, had changed but one thing remained the same for us both, the faithfulness of God.

You see, there is a place of peace. My journey although different from my mother's was actually very much the same. I learned from her what it means to have a relationship with Christ. I admired her strength and resilience in the most difficult situations. I loved her nurturing and loving spirit that caused so many spiritual daughters to connect with her and call her mom. And there were others in my life who helped me to grow as a woman. I will always be grateful for the opportunity to know other strong women who mentored and nurtured me along the way.

As you read this devotional, please open your heart and mind and allow God to speak to your situation. Sisters we are all different and the same. Although our struggles may differ our need for faith for the journey is the same. Meditate on the scriptures and apply them where you need them in your own life. If you have not accepted Jesus Christ as your Savior, I invite you to open your heart and let him in today. Let Him lead and guide your life. He does not promise that we will not have trials or storms, but He does promise to be with us through them all.

This devotional is my story. How as a daughter, sister, wife, mother of six, grandmother of two, pastor's wife, and pastor, I would not be who I am today without Christ in my life. My journey has not always been easy, but it has been fruitful. I have enjoyed many blessings along the way. Yes, the stories I tell are the truth of my life and how I have made it thus far. I am still on a journey and I am so grateful for the lessons I have learned. God has a purpose for my life, and he has created you for a purpose. Hold your head up and press on toward the goal. Become a woman of excellence, beauty, and grace. Enjoy the journey and remember God is there to guide you through it all.

CONTENTS

The Best Is yet to Come

For the Lord God is a sun and shield: the Lord will give grace and glory: no good thing will he withhold from them that walk uprightly.

(Psalm 84:11 KJV)

As I sit here today overcome with anxiety, I cannot see my way. Circumstances, most beyond my control, have caused distress. As my husband and I begin our morning devotions, he asks what's wrong and my answer is there are just so many things going on, and although I trust God, I'm just not sure how much longer He will allow this to continue. Can you identify with that? Sometimes we face one trial after another and although it may seem to never end, it will. God is with us, and as Psalm 84:11a KJV says, "For the Lord God is a sun and shield: The Lord will give grace and glory." God is with us when the sun is shining, and He is our shield when life is difficult.

Then, the question comes to my mind: do I *really* trust God? So, I Google trust and I am reminded that trust is the *firm* belief in the reliability, truth, ability, or strength of someone or something. Hmmm that's a strong definition. Do I rely on God? Do I believe the truth of

1

His word? Do I believe in His ability to come through for me? Do I believe in His ability to be my strength in my weakness? One thing is for sure sisters, tests and trials reveal what we truly believe.

As I sit there after our time of prayer and devotions, I am meditating on all of that. Then I turn on a TV show. The guest on the show today is a firm believer in combining spirituality with natural health. Wow, this sounds interesting, so I decide to watch. They mentioned the "m" word (menopause), but girl, that's another devotion for another day. Anyway, then the most amazing thing happened. At the end of the show, the guest says, "The best is yet to come." It is amazing to me in that moment because again, God knew exactly what I needed to hear. I began to say that to myself over and over. I got up from the couch where I was nursing my anxiety and meditating on *all* the things facing me, and I kept saying "the best is yet to come." Then I began to think on the word of God that is hidden in my heart for times just like these.

The following three scriptures came to mind immediately:

- "For I know the plans I have for you," declares the Lord, "plans to prosper you and not to harm you, plans to give you hope and a future." (Jeremiah 29:11 NIV)
- "Trust in the Lord with all thine heart; and lean not unto thine own understanding; In all your ways acknowledge him, and He shall direct thy paths." (Proverbs 3:5–6 KJV)
- "Give and it shall be given unto you; good measure, pressed down, and shaken together, and running over, shall men give into your bosom." (Luke 6:38a KJV)

I remember watching Pastor Robert Schuller on TV many years ago, and one thing he said often that I have never forgotten is "life's not fair, but God is good!" One of my favorite scriptures is 1 Peter 5:10 NIV. It reminds me that suffering is a part of the Christian journey. But it also lets me know that after I have suffered and endured the test, the result is that God himself will restore me and make me strong, firm, and steadfast. 1 Peter 4:12 NIV reminds us to not be surprised when the tests come as if it is something strange. 1 Peter 4:13 NIV says, "But rejoice inasmuch as you participate in the sufferings of Christ, so that you may be overjoyed when his glory is revealed." God's glory is revealed in us as we submit to Him as He is making us into the person we were created to be.

Psalm 84:5–7 NIV is a Psalm about the pilgrimage to Jerusalem. Verse 5 speaks of the joy of those whose strength comes from the Lord. Verse 6 says, "When they walk through the Valley of Weeping, it will become a place of refreshing springs. The autumn rains will clothe it with blessings." That is how life should be walking with God. We must remember that God is faithful, and each trial should increase our faith. No particular valley has been mentioned, so perhaps it symbolizes the struggles we will have as Christians. Yes, as we travel along this journey, we will have tears and joy. We must be sure that our struggles push us to and not away from God. Psalm 84:7 NIV, "says they go from strength to strength, till each appears before God in Zion." In the New Living Translation, Psalm 84:7 says, "They will continue to grow stronger, and each of them will appear before God in Jerusalem." As you go through your tests and trials, you should continue to grow stronger in God.

I was reading 2 Chronicles 20 NLT recently. Jehoshaphat was calling on the Lord because the enemy was bearing down on Judah. God spoke through Jahaziel with a message in verse 15: "He said, 'Listen, all you people of Judah and Jerusalem! Listen, King Jehoshaphat! This is what the Lord says: Do Not Be Afraid! Don't be discouraged by this mighty army, for the battle is not yours, but God's.'" Sisters, remember we must endure the difficult times to get to the best of times. So, girl, get up and stop nursing that anxiety and remember "the best is yet to come."

THE RIB OF ADAM

And the LORD God caused a deep sleep to fall upon Adam,
and he slept: and he took one of his ribs, and closed up the flesh
instead thereof; and the rib, which the Lord God had taken
from man, made he a woman, and brought her unto the man.

(GENESIS 2:21–22 KJV)

I love how God takes time to hear our prayers and reveal the answers
in such real-life situations. Years ago, I was seeking God for answers
to the question, how do I become a better wife? I had to determine
whether I really believed God chose me to be the wife my husband
needed. In that moment I realized I knew He did because of the reason
I married him. I married him because God said, "he is the one." Please
understand, I loved him very much, but it was a very conscious love,
meaning, I did not let myself get so caught up in the emotional part of
the relationship that I lost track of being conscious of the fact that I was
created for a specific man. I only wanted the man whose rib God used
specifically to make me (Genesis 2:22 KJV).

You see, when a man chooses the woman God has created to be his
wife, she is prepared specifically for that man. In that preparation, the

women is given all the tools and the wisdom she needs to love the man who chooses her (not the man that we choose). Proverbs 18:22 NIV says, "He who finds a wife finds what is good and receives favor from the Lord." We must know for sure we are saying yes to the man God has for us. So, when I talk to married women who are experiencing struggles, my first question is, do you truly believe God made you for him, and do you know you are truly his rib? Women marry for many different reasons, but there is a special connection when we know for sure he is the one. Marriage is a spiritual union that is not to be taken lightly. It is a beautiful journey together when God is leading the way.

When I go through difficult times (because they surely come for us all), I simply say to God, you knew on April 28, 1979, when I married my husband, that this day would come, so please tell me how to deal with this situation. The mistake we make is waiting until there is trouble to seek God. Yes, when there is difficulty, we must seek Him but also when things are going well. We want to be sure our marriage is always Christ-centered. Remember to include God in every decision as you build your life together.

I believe God chose me for my husband. I seek God daily in prayer and listen for His voice and instructions. We all have our individual roads to travel in marriage, and we cannot compare ourselves to others. God made us specifically for the husband we have. We must always remember that our husbands have struggles in life just as we do, and we must seek God for the root of that struggle and pray for them. During a particularly difficult time in my husband's life, I remember seeking God for direction. God told me He gave me to my husband because He knew He could trust me to walk through this pain with him and not leave him. While that was not exactly what I was expecting to hear at the time, it was very humbling. My tears flowed at the very thought that God would entrust someone so special to Himself to me. Can God trust you to walk through both the good and bad times with your husband? If we truly are *the one*, we can handle it. Seeking God during tough times and receiving our answers through prayer is what God desires of us.

Are you seeking God for the answers you need to be a Godly wife?

LAUGH

She is clothed with strength and dignity; she can laugh at the days to come.

(PROVERBS 31:25 NIV)

W hat does your calendar and to-do list look like? I remember the days of running a household of eight. I did not use a calendar and I did not miss a beat. There were no cell phones to alert me to the next task. I look back and think, wow, how did I do that?

Proverbs 31:25 NIV says she is clothed with strength. I believe if we ask, God will give us strength to accomplish everything we need to do. In Psalm 28:7 NLT, David says, "The Lord is my strength and shield. I trust him with all my heart." Too many times we rely on our own strength when God is just waiting for us to include Him so He may empower us with the strength we need for each new day.

The daily routine of a wife and/or mother may seem overwhelming. We must constantly consider the needs of others. If you are a caregiver, you too make great sacrifices that sometimes go unnoticed. But, remember the Lord is your strength and shield; trust Him with everything. With the Lord's strength, you can withstand much more pressure than you are able to on your own. A shield is for protection. The Lord is our protection and is looking out for us in ways that we may never know.

Although it can be overwhelming at times, our attitude regarding this awesome ministry we have been assigned by God takes us a long way. Seeing it as a blessing to be chosen for the job is a positive way to approach each day. If God has orchestrated your life in such a way that brought you to this season, He is trusting you to act with strength and dignity. Realizing the magnitude of your assignment should help you to understand the need to seek God daily for direction.

There is always a need to pray for your loved one no matter what season of life they are in. My mother birthed fourteen children, and she was so discerning and in tune with each of us that she would know when one of us was experiencing difficulty. She went to heaven at the age of ninety-two and was still concerned and praying for her children. When my father went to heaven, they had been married for fifty years. I witnessed how she stood by his side and prayed for him during his many years of ministry and through his illness. She also taught me to pray for my husband and children. Today I encourage you to develop a routine of praying for your loved ones, especially those you care for.

When we think about the Proverbs 31 woman, it is easy to become discouraged and think we can never do all of that. But the truth is you probably already do in your own way. Every woman's to-do list may look different from another, but we are all on the same journey.

The scripture verse today says she is clothed with strength and dignity and can laugh at the days to come. Laughing at the days to come is being free of anxiety and worry about the future. You may wonder, how in the world are you able to be free of anxiety and worry while dealing with crying babies or rebellious adolescents and teens all while working a full-time job? You may be experiencing a winter season in marriage or hardship on the job. How do I not worry about the future when so many things are ahead of me? The secret lies in the time you spend with God each day. Time spent with God is time well spent. Interceding in prayer on behalf of your husband and children (no matter what age) and others should not be optional. There is power in prayer, and as we are praying on their behalf, God is doing great things in their lives and protecting them from the hand of the enemy.

I remember getting up very early in the morning to read a scripture, talk to God about my day, and receive instruction. That was my time to cast all my cares on God and ask Him to direct all of my steps that day. Proverbs 31:25 NIV says she is clothed with strength and dignity. I too was clothed with strength and dignity, and so are you as you spend time with God. Imagine that time in the morning before the house begins to buzz with the start of the new day. You are up early clothing yourself with strength and dignity as you hear God's voice calling you to your secret place.

Sacrificing a few minutes of much-needed sleep to spend time with the one who is able to strengthen me was my secret to laughing at the days to come. Remember, Philippians 4:6 NIV tells us: "Do not be anxious about anything, but in every situation, by prayer and petition, with thanksgiving, present your requests to God." Thank God for your assignment. Tell Him all about it and let Him lead the way.

TAKE A NAP

The Lord is my shepherd, I lack nothing. He makes me lie down in green pastures, he leads me beside quiet waters, he refreshes my soul. He guides me along the right paths for his name's sake.

(PSALM 23:1–3 NIV)

I remember when my youngest sister was in college. One day she was overwhelmed and began to cry. My mother looked at my sister and said three words, "take a nap." I now understand that mom knew if we were going to learn to navigate through the storms of life, we needed to know where our help and strength lies. She knew that there would be times when the weight of the situation would seem unbearable. Just as the Good Shepherd knew, mom knew there was strength in rest.

Years later God revealed to me the wisdom in those three words. In Psalms 23 David said, "He makes me lie down in green pastures, he leads me beside quiet waters and refreshes my soul." God provides us opportunities to rest and refresh if we are in tune to His voice. The shepherd guides the sheep to green pastures, and in those green pastures, sheep rest and eat. Still waters are calm. When I think of green pastures and still waters, I think of resting in the arms of our savior. As we rest in His arms, He refreshes and restores us. One of the definitions Webster gives of restores is bringing back into a former or original state—to renew. Matthew 11:28 KJV says, "Come unto me, all ye that labor and are heavy laden, and I will give you rest." Rest is mentioned several times in scripture indicating it is a good thing to take time to do.

As women we face many stressful days. When all your responsibilities become overwhelming, take a nap. A synonym of nap is rest. A nap need not be in the middle of the day, it may be at any time you can find to pull away from everyone for a few minutes to refresh yourself. You don't need to sleep, just rest. Stop what you are doing, take deep breaths, and cast your anxiety on God. God is calling, come unto me.

I know you are thinking she must be kidding. But as the mother of six children, I can attest to what I am saying. There were many times I had to ask God to provide an opportunity for me to steal away and rest for just a few precious moments. How I accomplished that was different every time, but the bottom line is this: God knows our needs and will provide a way for us to rest. In the scripture, God as the Good Shepherd leads His children to rest in green pastures. Pour out your heart to Him when you are overwhelmed, and allow Him to lead you beside still waters and refresh your soul. Sometimes the dishes and laundry can wait, so you can refresh.

Oh, and by the way, after my sister took a nap, she woke up refreshed and received an A on the test!

I AM SOMEBODY SPECIAL

For you created my inmost being; you knit me together in my mother's womb.

I praise you because I am fearfully and wonderfully made; your works are wonderful, I know that full well.

(PSALM 139:13–14 NIV)

Have you ever experienced a time when it seemed like women all around you were doing great things? Then, that little voice inside your head says, "and you are only a ___." You fill in the blank. My blank was stay at home mom, which I preferred to call a domestic engineer. I had to remind myself that I am gifted and special and it is not based on who people say I am, but who God says I am.

In Psalms 139, David realizes God knows everything about him. "For you created my inmost being," that part deep within us that only God can see. David is taking time to acknowledge the intimacy we have with God from the very beginning of life. God had a plan for you from the beginning. David said, "you knit me together in my mother's womb." If you have ever attempted to knit, you know it is a very precise process. If the pattern is not followed exactly, you will not receive the desired result. Each project requires a different pattern and amount of time to complete. This is how our Heavenly Father created us. You were created on purpose with a specific plan and design for your life. David said, "I praise you because I am fearfully and wonderfully made." We must be careful to not entertain the lies Satan brings to us. Rejoice in the fact that you are fearfully and wonderfully made.

Once I realized what an honor it is to be chosen by God to be who I am, I was able to really declare, "your works are wonderful." I began to tell myself, "I am somebody special." Whatever God created you to be or do is an assignment specifically for you. He knit you together in your mother's womb with specific characteristics. Your skin color, your hair color, your personality, your strength, and your character were all fearfully and wonderfully made. Embrace who you are because you *are* somebody special created by Almighty God for a specific purpose.

And remember this, you are doing great things. Women are the unsung "sheroes" of this world. Just think about the many titles you hold simultaneously: chef, chauffeur, counselor, accountant, nurse, executive assistant, and the list goes on, many times, while also employed outside the home full-time and excelling in your career. I managed my household with the same energy I put into my career for years. Was I fulfilled? The answer to that is an unquestionable yes. God's works are wonderful, and I know that fully well! I knew I was doing what I was called to in that season.

Success is not measured in dollars and cents. Remember to measure your success by the goals you have accomplished. Allow God to take control and lead you down the path He has planned for your life. Remember, you have a purpose, and as you spend time with God in prayer and His word, that purpose will be revealed. Take time to reminisce and thank God for the accomplishments great and small. Many times, we don't realize what God has done because we do not take time to stop and think about the big and small goals we have accomplished. I have journaled my goals for many years and I am in awe when I go back and read and realize that although I may have forgotten, God did not. I see how many obstacles I have overcome and how much I have accomplished by the grace of God. In this season of my life, I see how everything has worked together so that God may be glorified in my life.

You are special to God. There will be seasons of discouragement and disappointment, but keep pressing toward your goals. The important thing is to include God in your plans and follow His lead. Sister, remember to remind yourself often that you *are* somebody special!

Don't Worry About It

Do not be anxious about anything, but in every situation, by prayer and petition, with thanksgiving, present your requests to God. And the peace of God, which transcends all understanding, will guard your hearts and your minds in Christ Jesus.

(Philippians 4:6–7 NIV)

As women we sometimes worry too much. We want things to be perfect for our husbands and children and even for ourselves. When Jesus was speaking to the disciples, He reminded them that in this world, we will have trouble, but we should find peace in the one who has overcome the world. He says, "I have told you these things, so that in me you may have peace. In this world you will have trouble. But take heart! I have overcome the world" (John 16:33 NIV).

In Philippians, the scripture tells us not to be anxious for anything but to make our requests known to God. What is the thing that causes you the most sleepless nights? Whatever it is, take it to God in prayer. God knows our thoughts even before we think them; but talking to

Him about it is a way of releasing it to Him. God is the one who orchestrates our lives and sets things in motion.

I was attending a women's breakfast at my church and the speaker that day was the founder of a Christian academy. I had never heard of her before that day. While she was teaching, she walked over to me and took my hand and said, "God said you will not have to worry about your children getting through college." At that time, none of my six children were even in high school, but I thanked God for that promise and forgot about it until the time came for them to go to college.

Through every struggle I reminded God of his words to me that day and I did not worry. Today, all of our six children have graduated college. She did not say they would receive full scholarships; she said I will not have to worry. Were there difficult times for them? Yes. But I remembered her words that I should not worry.

Sometimes in our zeal to give our children the best and not allow them to go without (perhaps as we did), we interfere with God's work in their lives. I had the peace of God that Paul spoke of in Philippians 4:7 and allowed God to do His work in my children's lives. The result of those struggles during their college days is a closer walk with God, because they too had to have faith to make it through the tough times.

Anxiety is worrying or feeling nervous or uneasy about a situation. We are anxious because we do not know how the situation will turn out. Note that the scripture today did not say God will immediately solve the issue you are anxious about; although He is able to, it says He will give you peace, freedom from worry, and calm. To have peace in the storm is the gift God offers in this scripture. The scripture says peace that transcends all understanding. Peace that goes beyond our level of understanding is what God promises.

Whatever you are facing today, don't worry about it. God knows what you need and is waiting for you to trust Him and rest in His care.

LETTING GO

And we know that all things work together for good to those
who love God, to those who are the called according to His
purpose.

(ROMANS 8:28 NKJV)

M y son was complaining about pain around his ribcage. Not in
agony, but it had become a constant complaint. I took him to
the pediatrician, and the doctor decided that he should have tests since
he had complained about the pain a few times. The doctor thought
it may be growing pains along with my son lifting weights, possibly
heavier than he should. At that time my son was thirteen years old and
was a very active and talented athlete running track and wrestling.

On the day of the cardiology visit, everything seemed to be going
well. The cardiologist examined him and did an EKG and found no
cause for alarm but wanted to do an echocardiogram just to be on the
safe side. The technician assured us we would be out of the office in
twenty minutes. He let us know he had been doing echocardiograms
for twenty-two years and they don't take long. Well, two hours later
we were still there. Something was very strange. He could not find my

son's left coronary artery. We left the doctor's office still unsure of what that all meant, but we knew there was a problem.

When the pediatrician received the results, he called, and the news wasn't good. My son was to discontinue all physical activity *immediately*. How do I break this news to an active thirteen-year old who was a track star and wrestler? Well I did, and he was very mature in handling the news. He decided to focus more on music. He wasn't an accomplished musician; he just had an interest. We had no idea at that time that music was his destiny. We couldn't see then how God would use him in ways we could not imagine. We didn't know that God would use him to offer his gift to bless churches that did not have a musician or could not afford one. It all worked together for his good.

In Romans 8:28 NKJV, the Apostle Paul says, "and we know that ALL things work together for good to those who love God." Do you love God? Is He a part of your daily life? Do you trust Him with your life? The second part of the verse says, "to those who are the called according to His purpose." This promise is for believers, those who love Him and are living according to His will and commandments.

How do you handle life when you need to let go? Do you wrestle or rest? Do you realize God may have a better plan or may be moving you or your loved one closer to the plan and purpose for your life? I marveled at how easily my son just let it go. I learned something from Him that day: don't wait or hesitate. Today, he is a gifted child, a talented musician with a beautiful sincere heart who is loved by so many. And sixteen years later, he still pauses on the anniversary of his open-heart surgery to give thanks to God for what He did for him. I will be forever grateful to him for the lessons I learned in my own walk with God during such a difficult time in my son's life. He is the youngest of six and his situation affected the entire family. I learned that all things good and bad truly do work together for good. And, I learned that we should not live a life that causes us to bargain with God when trouble comes. We should love God with all our heart daily and always pursue His purpose for our lives.

I faced a situation recently that was very challenging because the outcome could be life-changing. At a point where I felt myself fighting for myself, I had to pause and remind myself that God is in control. I had to recite Romans 8:28 and let it saturate my spirit until I could let it go. I had to remind myself that I love God and I am the called according to His purpose. You see my sister, when we trust God, we can let it go knowing He will work it out for our good. I was seeking the answer that I believed would work for me, but God knows my future. Only when we let go do we see the hand of God in our situation. God always has a plan.

PRESSING ON

And Moses said unto the people, Fear ye not, stand still, and
see the salvation of the Lord, which he will shew to you today;
for the Egyptians whom ye have seen today, ye shall see them
again no more forever. The Lord shall fight for you, and ye
shall hold your peace.

(EXODUS 14:13–14 KJV)

Sometimes the situations we find ourselves in are so bizarre that we
lose focus for a moment. We want to run away from the pain, not
realizing the pain is temporary, and for me it was all a part of God's
plan. Trials make us stronger and help us grow in our spiritual walk.
When we are able to see the hand of God in what sometimes seems like
a hopeless situation, we feel His love and reassurance that everything
will be okay.

As I write today, I am sitting in the recliner where I have slept for
ten days with an immobilizer on my arm. I'm asking God to help me
make it through this test. I think, "okay God, surgery and recovery are
enough, but now this too?" I'm asking God to give me peace as I wrestle against what I perceive as an injustice against me. And as I hear Him

on this very early morning and begin to reach for each of the items, He tells me to gather; He does what He often does. He chooses the songs I need to hear on my shuffled worship list, He tells me to begin to read a book given to me by a good friend, and He takes me back to my first devotional I wrote several years ago. What happens next is what should happen when we are open to Holy Spirit. Through my tears, my spirit calms and my eyes are opened to the enemy's devices. Of course, my flesh is at war with my spirit and still wants to win; it's the job of the enemy to change my focus. But I am reminded that I am to focus on the positive. Oh yes, whatever is true, honorable, right, pure, lovely, and of good report, dwell on these things! The truth is if we can manage to do that, it really works.

In my current state of mind, fear sets in. I feel like I'm being consumed by this situation. I feel helpless and alone. To say it hurts is an understatement. Then I remember Moses as he led the Israelites in Exodus. This is a great story of how God has the power to deliver us from the enemy's hand. "Fear not, stand still" are such powerful words. Do you know the story? If not, you should read the book of Exodus. The bottom line is that God uses Moses to deliver His people Israel from the terrible injustice of a fearless leader named Pharaoh. There were many times when the Israelites were afraid and couldn't see how things were going to work out and Moses had to remind them that God is the one who is fighting the battle, so all they needed to do was stand still and see the salvation of the Lord. That statement was true for me that day. Sisters, some battles are just too big for us to fight. We know that we should depend on God for everything; and as we learn to allow Him to fight the small battles, we see His salvation and our faith grows for the big ones.

Obeying Holy Spirit will require some humility on my part, but I am reminded of the scripture in James 4:10 NLT that says, "when you bow down before the Lord and admit your dependence on him, he will lift you up and give you honor." Isaiah 58:8 NLT says, "if you do these things, your salvation will come like the dawn. Yes, your healing will come quickly. Your godliness will lead you forward, and the glory of the Lord will protect you from behind." It is very difficult to obey when we are hurt or wronged. It takes humility to place the situation in God's hands, but the scripture is clear on the benefits.

Finally, in Philippians 3:13 NIV, Paul admits that he is not perfect, but choosing to forget the past, he presses forward to the main goal. Paul didn't say move forward, he said press. Pressing is moving with determination, pressing through obstacles. As I press on in His will, may His glory be revealed in me. Yes, my desire is that God's presence be manifested in my life and decisions. Forgetting those things which are behind, I'm pressing on. What about you?

Your Steps Are Ordered

The Lord directs the steps of the godly. He delights in every detail of their lives.

(PSALM 37:23 NLT)

It is very interesting to look back and reflect on my life. I am truly grateful for the opportunities and doors God opened for me. My memories of being a wife and mother warm my heart as I remember all the good times with immediate and extended family. I am the twelfth of fourteen children, and I am blessed with six children of my own. Our home was always open to family and I truly was the happy hostess.

Ministry was also a blessing as I was able to assist my husband and many great women in ministry, mostly pastors' wives whose excellent leadership propelled me into a women's ministry of my own. My career took off in a totally unexpected way that I now realize was a setup by God for greater things in ministry. So, why do I sit and ponder today wondering what I have done with my life and what's next?

As the years progress, the day comes when you realize you have more years behind you than before you and you want to make them *all* count. As I am reading this morning, I come across Psalm 37:23 NLT, and it says, "the Lord directs the steps of the godly"—the godly, the one who believes, trusts, and obeys. Yes, my steps are ordered, so how will the years before me unfold? One step at a time! After all, steps take you to a higher level and are a part of the process. It is interesting that most people opt to take an elevator or escalator because it is easier than climbing stairs. Elevators and escalators are the faster way and we want to get to the top as quickly and as easily as possible.

But today I have made the decision that I will keep climbing each step one at a time, facing each challenge, enjoying every victory, and walking through every door God opens as I fulfill my destiny. Then, one day I will take that one last step into the arms of my Lord and Savior to hear the words that I'm working toward, "well done my daughter, welcome home."

Your steps too are ordered, so my sister, skip the elevator and escalator, and take the stairs. You don't want to miss anything on the way to your destiny. Embrace every open door and opportunity along the way. Your steps are ordered!

Still Shaking My Head

Train up a child in the way he should go: and when he is old,
he will not depart from it.

(PROVERBS 22:6 KJV)

I cannot tell you how many times people wanted to declare me insane
for having six children. They would say things like, your life is not
your own, I bet you never get any sleep, and I'm sure you are always
broke. I decided to take it as pity rather than rudeness. But there was
no reason to pity me or feel sorry for me because I was living my best
life. I asked God for every one of them. Six beautiful, unique, gifted
little people who have, by the way, grown into six extraordinary adults
that my husband and I are very proud of.

So, you may ask, how in the world did I do it? And my answer is by
establishing order. My husband and I were a great team and the perfect
balance of what our children needed. He was the spiritual leader, and I
was second-in-command. My husband never ceased to feed us spiritually. We had our own weekly bible study, and let me tell you they were
fun. We opened our home to children in the family and neighborhood
and shared our faith with them. We were also blessed to give each of

our children some years of education in Christian schools. So spiritual order was definitely established.

But there is also a need for children to learn responsibility, and my job was to establish order in the home. I woke up every day with a plan, an agenda. There were days when the plan was no plan. But in all seriousness, my household was my purpose during those years, and I took it very seriously. There were expectations, there were chores, there were rewards, and there was discipline. We were a family and we were all expected to participate. No one was exempt. Everyone knew what was expected of them. One of my favorite times was family meetings where everyone was able to respectfully share their opinions and suggestions. We also had family court to settle disputes. Children understand more than we give them credit for. Including them helped them to learn communication and problem-solving skills that would be necessary as they ventured into the world as young adults.

So, you see, there are many levels to establishing order. Are you training your child(ren) in the way they should go as the Bible says? I can attest to the fact that if you follow this biblical principle, when they leave the nest, their physical body may be gone but their spirit will not depart from your training. By the way, all six of mine called home from college to say, "thanks mom."

Yes, I am actually still shaking my head at some of the comments I had to endure. I meet mothers today who have been told the same things. But I would not change my decision. If you have children, hold your head high and understand that you have been chosen by God to nurture and train them. Invite God into every situation and decision you face concerning them, and allow Him to lead the way.

DON'T GIVE UP

That is why we never give up. Though our bodies are dying,
our spirits are being renewed every day.

(2 CORINTHIANS 4:16 NLT)

I was having one of those mornings. We all have them. This was a
morning when I was just drained. I was working on a certification
and really pushing to get everything done on time. I knew finishing
the course could have a great impact on my career, but I was tired and
wanted to quit. Should I just give up and accept defeat, I wondered.
Then I had my morning prayer and devotions. All three devotions I
chose to read that morning said the exact same thing in different ways:
don't give up!

The first seven words I read said, "that is why we never give up" (2
Corinthians 4:16 NLT). Then I read a devotional from Dr. Tony Evans
and the title was "Focus on Jesus, the Alpha and Omega." Then he said,
"friend, I know you are probably tired right now." And finally, I picked
up my reading from a book by Bishop Jakes called *Destiny*, and the
page I was to read next said, "ordering your life takes time."

We all may have times when it seems like we are working so hard or trying to do the right things to be successful and not getting anywhere. Life is a journey full of different seasons, and as we know, each season brings something unique. Even the seasons of nature, summer, spring, fall, and winter, are unique. I find it interesting when conversing with friends and family how each person has a favorite season. I don't like winter at all, but I know people who love it.

I have been through all seasons. My story is truly full of summer, spring, fall, and winter. But I realize it took all of that to make me who I am today. Winter is my most difficult season, but reflecting on a winter season in my life, and realizing it is now just a memory and I'm still here, gives me the strength to get up and keep moving. I didn't quit, and I didn't give up. Although my outer man was tired, I pulled on my inner strength. That's what Paul meant in 2 Corinthians 4:16. Paul knew personally what it meant to suffer, and that is why he exhorts us in Ephesians 6:10 KJV to be strong in the Lord and in the power of His might. He knew we would eventually need to draw on that inner strength obtained from a consistent relationship with God through prayer and studying His word. Ephesians 6:11 KJV tells us to put on the whole armor of God that we may be able to stand against the wiles of the devil. Yes, my sister, just as we put on coats to protect our physical body from the harsh cold of winter, we put on the armor of God to protect us spiritually.

Winter is when the ground freezes and growth ceases. It is cold and there is snow, ice, and hibernation. But, a very miraculous thing is happening during the winter season called preparation. The ground is soaking up the water from the snow and ice to keep the roots in the ground nourished in preparation for spring. Spring is when nature begins to bloom and blossom. When we see the flowers begin to bud and the trees begin to turn from brown to green, we know spring is on the way. Do you get the picture? Allow God to saturate you during your winter season. In the stillness and loneliness you may feel during your storm, know that He is preparing you for something greater, so don't give up! Abide in His word and in prayer and just wait.

As 2 Corinthians 4:16 NLT says, "though this body may be tired, my spirit is being renewed daily." And that's why I'm not giving up. I love the words to the song Bishop Paul S. Morton sings, "I'm Still Standing." I'm still standing, I'm still trusting, I'm still holding on to what I believe. Still motivated, fully persuaded, I'm still standing on the word that's in my heart.

Sister, will you stand with me? Don't give up!

TRUST

He cuts off every branch of mine that doesn't produce fruit,
and he prunes the branches that do bear fruit so they will produce even more fruit.

(JOHN 15:2 NLT)

H ave you ever observed landscapers prepare a yard during the
spring season? Just from observing, sometimes it appears as if
they are doing more damage than good. They begin to pull away dead
leaves and sometimes even remove entire branches. Before you know
it, there may seem to be more in the dead pile than left on the bush or
tree. But, pruning soon reveals whether that bush or tree will live or
die. A healthy fruit tree will continue to bear fruit. A healthy flower
bush will bloom once again because everything that is dead has been
removed. The key is for the owner to trust that the landscaper knows
what to do and when. If an owner were to neglect their landscape,
it doesn't always mean the fruit or flowers will not come forth, but
neglect will surely slow down or hinder the process. The owner must
be open to whatever needs to be done to produce growth.

In the book of John, Jesus teaches us about bearing fruit. The scripture says, "he cuts off every branch of mine that doesn't produce fruit." We all know cutting hurts. Being pruned is difficult as it requires cutting and removing what is dead in our lives. Sometimes we don't realize that our inability to let things go can cause us to become stagnant and cease to grow spiritually. Through the pain of what I thought was "losing," I learned about spiritual pruning. In the beginning, the process was very painful as I did not understand what was happening. But as I began to "trust" God more, it became easier to recognize His process and believe what was happening was for my good. Believe me, pruning is never easy, but the healing process can be so much better if you trust the person caring for you.

One of my favorite devotionals is *Secrets of the Vine* by Bruce Wilkerson. One of the many chapters in the book is entitled "Making Room for MORE." In that chapter he explains how God is repeatedly pruning us to make room for more fruit in our lives. We may be bearing some fruit, but if we are still being pruned, that means there is room for more fruit. Another lesson I learned through my personal pruning process is that sometimes things we enjoy are also cut away. That was really painful for me, but I realized the season was just over and God was moving me on to a place where I can be more fruitful.

In the natural, a vine may have some fruit such as small grapes still visible and growing, but that does not mean they are healthy. They may be struggling to grow because of all of the unhealthy dead bushes and so on surrounding them. Once the unhealthy shrubs and brush are removed, it allows for healthy growth, beautiful, large, juicy grapes that are no longer hindered. Are you in an unhealthy environment that is hindering your spiritual growth? You may be growing, but as the second part of John 15:2 NLT says, "and he prunes the branches that

DO bear fruit so they will produce even more." The goal is to bear fruit, and then more fruit, and then much fruit. This is a process.

Are you experiencing pruning and having a painful experience right now? Let me encourage you to trust God. As He removes all the things in your life that hinder fruit bearing, you will begin to bloom like a beautifully landscaped garden full of fruit and flowers. God knows exactly who and what we need in order to grow. Pruning is a time of testing. James 1:3 NIV reminds us that the testing of our faith produces perseverance. Galatians 5:22–23 NIV gives us a list of spiritual fruit that we will produce as we are pruned by God.

Remember to trust God as you are being prepared to bear fruit, *more* fruit, and *much* fruit. Think about the words to the song, "I Surrender All," and as the old saying goes, just let go and let God.

Making It Count

So be careful how you live. Don't live like fools, but like those who are wise.

Make the most of every opportunity in these evil days. Don't act thoughtlessly, but understand what the Lord wants you to do.

(Ephesians 5:15–17 NLT)

Ephesians tells us to be careful how we live and to be wise, making the best use of our time. We are also to know what the will of the Lord is. Time flies and it's something we cannot get back once it is gone. Every morning we receive a new twenty-four-hour bank of time, and if we don't use it, it is just gone. Did you ever consider that? Imagine if that were money in the bank. How many thousands of dollars would have been lost?

Lamentations 3:22–23 KJV says, "It is of the Lord's mercies that we are not consumed, because his compassions fail not. They are new every morning: great is thy faithfulness." We awaken to new mercies every morning. I love the scripture and song by Dave Hunt that says "the steadfast love of the Lord never ceases, his mercies never come to an end." They are new every morning, great is thy faithfulness. Every morning we receive new mercy from God and another twenty-four-hour bank of time to make it count.

Our morning should begin by asking God for wisdom and to guide our footsteps. As I reflect, I remember times of frustration when I was running late or had to change my schedule or route only to end up exactly where God intended me to be—the place where He needed to use me to help or encourage someone else that day.

Be determined to make it count. Don't waste time on things or people who are not helping you to fulfill your purpose and grow in Christ. Allow God to order your steps daily. Let go of old habits that are not a part of the plan: behaviors that weigh you down and old mindsets and strongholds that hinder your growth. Make the most of every opportunity. Are you meeting that friend for coffee every day at 8:05am to gossip, or does she have something to contribute to move you a step forward in your life and faith? Is lunch with that coworker just a habit and time to catch up on the latest happenings in the office, or can you use that hour for quiet time to read the Bible or listen to something uplifting?

In the book of Ephesians, Paul is writing to God's people in Ephesus. The first verse in chapter 5 exhorts us to imitate God in everything we do. We need to have a standard as Christians. Just like it was then, we are still living in a world where there is evil, so we should always be mindful of our actions and behaviors. We need to be sure our lights shine in the darkness.

"Order my steps in your word Lord and lead and guide me daily" should be your prayer. Remember to make every minute count because we cannot get that minute back once it is gone.

Embracing the Plan

The Lord will work out his plans for my life—for your faithful love, O Lord, endures forever. Don't abandon me, for you made me.

(Psalm 138:8 NLT)

The Lord will work out His plans for my life. The same verse in KJV says, "the Lord will perfect that which concerneth me." As I began to look at the word perfect, the verb form said make better or improve. But my favorite definition is to fine-tune. To fine-tune means to make small adjustments in order to achieve the best or desired performance.

As we embrace God's plan, that is exactly what He does. The more we grow, the more we know. As we wind through the many phases and seasons of life, God is constantly fine-tuning us for the next step, level, or season. That is if we include Him in our plans. The theme of Psalm 138 is thanksgiving for answered prayer. This is a beautiful Psalm. David starts with "I give you thanks, O Lord, with all my heart." Verse 3 NLT says, "as soon as I pray you answer me; you encourage me by giving me strength." In the final verse 8, David says, "the Lord will work out his plans for my life." God must be a part of our plans if we want to succeed. He knows what we desire and is able to help us fulfill our dreams.

The definition said small adjustments. If you look back and reflect on your gift, calling, and purpose, you should see how much you have grown. The process of perfecting us brings about growth. The process of growth involves pruning which is a painful process. It involves stepping out of your comfort zone which is a fearful process. And it involves walking through new doors to experience new things which is a hopeful process. After all, feeling hopeful is inspiring optimism about a future event. Hebrews tells us faith is the substance of things hoped for.

To embrace means to accept willingly and enthusiastically. We like to quote Jeremiah 29:11 NLT that says, "For I know the plans I have for you says the Lord." But are you embracing the plan? On your journey to destiny, do you have your own plan, or are you in tune with God's plan for your life?

Don't prolong the journey with wrong turns. Many times, what God wants us to do may seem unachievable. There have been so many times that I could not see myself as God sees me. God just keeps fine-tuning me. He's making small adjustments along the way. He's making me better. He's making improvements. He is perfecting that which concerns me. That which concerns me is the responsibility He has given me, my ministry.

My sister, embrace your calling and allow God to fine-tune you to do great things in your life.

FINDING THE BRIGHT SIDE

In every thing give thanks: for this is the will of God in Christ
Jesus concerning you.

(1 THESSALONIANS 5:18 KJV)

L ife brings situations that will cause us to become discouraged at
times. Sickness, death, financial struggles, marital problems, dis-
obedient children, and difficult relationships are just a few of the many
situations we face.

As women, our busy schedules and situations do not always allow
us to just stop and grieve, stay in bed with a minor illness, or get another
job to help with finances. We can't crumble under the pain of disobedi-
ent children or a marriage that seems to be failing. We sometimes feel
like the weight of the family is on our shoulders. So, what do we do?

First Thessalonians 5:18 KJV tells us in every thing to give thanks.
Paul writes to the church in Thessalonica to encourage them and
admonish them to be strong in their faith. The scripture did not say
for all things, but *in* all things. I am a witness that there is a bright side
in the darkest situations. In Deuteronomy 31:7 NIV, Moses encourages
Joshua to be strong and courageous. The scripture says, "Then Moses

summoned Joshua and said to him in the presence of all Israel, 'Be strong and courageous, for you must go with this people into the land that the Lord swore to their ancestors to give them.'" He told him not to be afraid or discouraged because "The Lord himself will lead you and be with you; he will never leave you nor forsake you." He did not tell Joshua there will not be trouble or adversity; he told him to be courageous and to remember God is with him. That is what we do, sisters. We stand strong and believe that God sees and knows the load we carry and will soon send relief. Remain fervent in prayer, fast when necessary, and quote His word. Ephesians tells us to put on the whole armor as we stand against the devices of the devil. Satan is always on his job oppressing and discouraging, but we have victory through Jesus Christ.

Jesus already told us in His word in John 16:33 NIV that "in this world we will have trouble." But, we are to be encouraged knowing He has already overcome the world. And because of this, we are also overcomers. In your darkest hour, think of something to be thankful for. Remember, adversity tests our faith and the more we overcome, the stronger we become. As you become quiet and humble before God, He will guide you through the most difficult situations. Prayer is the greatest weapon we have in those seemingly insurmountable situations.

Philippians 4:8 NLT tells us to think positive thoughts, thoughts that are true, honorable, right, pure, lovely, and admirable. Ask God to help you focus on good things when bad things happen. Always find the bright side.

My Help

Psalm 121 KJV

There are times when I wonder how I make it through some of the situations I experience. As I sit quietly today, I am grateful for my relationship with God. I'm grateful for Holy Spirit to lead and guide me daily. I am grateful for the Lord… my help.

My meditation today is Psalm 121. This Psalm is only 8 verses but is full of powerful words. This psalm was a song for pilgrims ascending to Jerusalem. The author is anonymous but knows the power of looking to God for help. As we travel through what can sometimes seem like a long journey, this psalm reminds us that our help comes from the Lord. It is a song of protection. We are protected by the hand of God as we journey through any situation if we live for and trust in Him.

Psalm 121 KJV:
1. I will lift up mine eyes unto the hills, from whence cometh my help.
2. My help cometh from the Lord, which made heaven and earth.

3. He will not suffer thy foot to be moved: he that keepeth thee will not slumber.
4. Behold, he that keepeth Israel shall neither slumber nor sleep.
5. The Lord is thy keeper: the Lord is thy shade upon thy right hand.
6. The sun shall not smite thee by day, nor the moon by night.
7. The lord shall preserve thee from all evil: he shall preserve thy soul.
8. The Lord shall preserve thy going out and thy coming in from this time forth, and even for evermore.

The word "help" means to make it easier for someone to accomplish something by offering one's services or resources. We are all called to do something. We have been placed on this earth for a purpose. God has offered us resources to help make what seems impossible easier. Prayer and the Bible are two resources God has given to help us navigate through life's journey. He has also given us other Christians so there is no need to feel alone.

Why not take this moment to lift up your eyes to the one from whom all of your help comes? Looking to the hills is to look past people and things that may offer promises or exalt themselves above God as what you need to solve your problems or get to the place you are striving to be. Come before Him holding back nothing. Pour out your heart and soul before Him. He shall preserve thee from all evil. He shall preserve thy soul. The sun shall not smite thee by day nor the moon by night. Remember He never slumbers or sleeps. He is the creator of all things. He holds the resources to everything you need.

My sister, find confidence and peace in knowing all that you need is in the Lord. All of my help cometh from the Lord.

A Servant's Heart

The greatest among you will be your servant.

(MATTHEW 23:11 NIV)

Matthew 23:11 says, "The greatest among you will be your servant." In Matthew 23, Jesus was teaching and warning against the attitudes of religious leaders of that day. Jesus was teaching leaders to serve others rather than to have others serve them.

In today's society, celebrity status is celebrated. It's sad to say this is not only going on in the world, but also in the church. People strive for leadership positions to be seen and feel important. Jesus was teaching against this in Matthew. Jesus said the teachers of religious laws and the Pharisees didn't practice what they taught but did everything for show. He said they love to wear religious garments, they sit at head tables at banquets and in special seats in the synagogue, and they love to receive respectful greetings. Sound familiar?

Matthew 23:11 NIV says, "The greatest among you will be your servant." A servant is a devoted and helpful follower or supporter. To serve is to think of others rather than yourself. It takes humility to serve rather than be served. Verse 12 lets us know "For those who exalt

49

themselves will be humbled and those who humble themselves will be exalted."

There is satisfaction in serving others. We never lose when we serve. Serving is the secret to being blessed. Take time today to think of ways you may serve others. Will you give of your time, treasure, or talent? There are so many ways to be a blessing to others. Don't forget to look outside the four walls of the church. Yes, serving in ministry is important, but so is serving our husbands, children, and others around us in need. Remember, we don't seek greatness, but it comes from serving with humility and a heart for others. You may not see greatness as the world shows, but you will be great in the eyes of God.

As I write today, I think of all the years I have served and the joy that comes from seeing others succeed. My focus is always on pleasing God and building His kingdom as I offered my time, talent, and treasure in service. Hebrews 6:10 NIV says, "God is not unjust; he will not forget your work and the love you have shown him as you have helped his people and continue to help them." If you are serving and feel unappreciated and discouraged, remember those times may come, but don't stay there. I believe God knew those we serve may not always show appreciation, so the writer of Hebrews reminds us that God sees the work we do in the kingdom. God is able to reward you in ways no man can match. Hold your head up and continue to offer your very best to the kingdom of God.

Sister, whenever you get discouraged, read Colossians 3:23–24 NIV: "Whatever you do, work at it with all your heart, as working for the Lord, not for human masters, since you know that you will receive an inheritance from the Lord as a reward. It is the Lord Christ you are serving."

JUST WAIT

But they that wait upon the Lord shall renew their strength;
they shall mount up with wings as eagles; they shall run, and
not be weary; and they shall walk, and not faint.

(ISAIAH 40:31 KJV)

Waiting is a process most people do not like. We live in a society where we want things and we want them *now*. Yet, it is interesting that we spend so much of our day waiting. We wait in grocery or department stores, doctors' offices, car service centers, traffic, and more. Many times, our eyes are constantly shifting from line to line or lane to lane for a way to move ahead. Or we are frequently asking how much longer we must wait. It appears waiting goes against our very nature, so it is interesting that Isaiah encouraged us by letting us know that waiting renews our strength.

Isaiah prophesied for many years. In the first thirty-nine chapters, he is crying out to Israel and the surrounding nations to repent of their sins. In Isaiah 40 he begins to comfort them and prophesy of the promising future through the coming Messiah. Isaiah writes of the majesty of God as he reunites Israel and Judah after exile. The chapter begins in verse one with "Comfort ye, comfort ye my people, saith your God." As you read through the chapter, notice Isaiah's message to the people to not only repent, but to be renewed. Isaiah says in verse 30, "Even the youths shall faint and be weary, and the young men shall utterly fall." Isaiah knew the process of life can cause us to become weary. Then, in Isaiah 40:31 KJV, the prophet Isaiah says, "But they that wait upon the Lord shall renew their strength; they shall mount up on wings as eagles." Eagles soar high into the sky. To soar is to fly or rise high in the air. The key to an eagle rising high is finding a strong wind current to raise them up. They wait and once they connect with that current, they are able to soar to great heights. When storms come, eagles embrace the strong winds of a storm and fly above the clouds, while most birds find a hiding place

It is not uncommon for even the strongest Christians to grow weary at times. Life can throw one blow after another and wear us down. The word "but" is how verse 31 begins. Hold up, wait a minute, there's more to come. Remember verse 30 tells us even youths will faint and be weary. I find that interesting considering the scripture in 1 John 2:14 KJV that speaks of young men being strong. The writer of Hebrews lets us know that even the strong become weak at times. *But if we trust in the Lord, He will give us new strength!*

Colossians 3:2 NKJV tells us to set our minds on things above, not on things on the earth. In order to do that, we must rise above the anxious thoughts of those things we are awaiting and keep our eyes on Christ. The eagle knows what awaits if she can just break through the storm clouds. How are you surviving the storm, are you hiding it out with the ravens and vultures, or are you riding the storm like an eagle, finding a strong wind, spreading your wings, and soaring above the dark clouds?

We must use prayer and the word of God to feed our minds positive, encouraging thoughts while we wait. Let go of anything that is dead in your life. Stop feeding your mind those things that don't give nourishment. If you want to soar, forget past hurts and disappointments. These things will only weigh you down. Start every day with a fresh new mindset. Feed on scriptures specific to your need and situation.

Some of the best advice I received as a young woman was to learn to rise above it. And today, I am going to add, rise above it "and just wait." God will either change the situation or change you for the situation.

Lift Your Head

But thou, o Lord, art a shield for me; my glory, and the lifter
up of mine head.

(Psalm 3:3 KJV)

I was driving along listening to Victoria Osteen live and the guest on
the show that day said she studied behavioral science in college, and
among other body languages she mentioned, she said a hung down
head is a sign of defeat. I just said wow. I knew it meant a person may
be sad or discouraged, but I never thought of feeling defeated.

It caused me to think back on different times in my life when I was
feeling down. I tried to remember if at those times I hung my head.
And yes, there were times when I hung my head. What about you?
When the financial plan does not come together, when marriage seems
off course and you can't see how you will make it, when children are
doing everything opposite of what you taught them, when friends walk
away and you don't know why, when you are certain you will be chosen
for a new position but it goes to someone else, or when you receive a
call from the doctor with bad news, do you hang your head in defeat?

To feel defeated is to feel like you have lost the battle. It does not feel good to lose anything but losing is a part of life. We suffer loss when anything we love in our lives leaves or is taken away. Loss causes us to grieve. We don't just grieve when someone dies but at other times of loss as well. Psalm 3:3 KJV says, "But thou oh Lord, art a shield for me; my glory and the lifter up of mine head." During this time, David was on the run and fearing for his life. Although David had an army that was able to protect him and help him defeat Absalom, he chose to trust God and he was at peace. David said God was his glory. God was David's security and the one with all power. God was the one who caused David to lift his head.

When you feel defeated by your circumstances, lift your head and trust God, not man. No matter who or what is coming against you today, remember God is your help. Remember God knows you and He wrote your life story. He alone is the lifter of your head. Because God sent His son to the cross, Satan is already defeated, and we are victorious.

If you are broken in spirit today and feel surrounded by defeat, lift up your head and begin to worship God. Read Psalm 24:7 KJV as you worship, and allow the King of glory to fill your temple. Verse 8 says, "Who is the King of glory? The Lord strong and mighty, the Lord mighty in battle." Lift up your head and allow the sweet peace and joy of the Lord to come in. The battle belongs to the Lord: *lift your head!*

Making Decisions

When you pass through the waters, I will be with you; and
when you pass through the rivers, they will not sweep over
you. When you walk through the fire, you will not be burned;
the flames will not set you ablaze.

(Isaiah 43:2 NIV)

Life brings so many challenges, so many decisions to make daily.
From the time we open our eyes in the morning, we are making decisions. Think about it, even small things like *should I get up
now or sleep a bit longer* is a decision. *What shall I wear today*, another
decision. Some decisions require a simple yes or no answer while others require more thought. As I was planning my day and looking at
some of the decisions I needed to make, Isaiah 43:2 NIV came to my
mind. One, because it is one of my favorite verses, so it comes to mind
often; but also because all of the situations mentioned remind me that
it doesn't matter what I am about to go through, God is there. All God
wants is an invitation and He will be with us through everything. The
elements mentioned in this verse can drown you or burn you if you

rely on your own strength. But look at God's promise to Israel, despite all that had already happened, God still wanted to show them mercy.

When we become Christians, we make a decision to follow Christ and become one of His disciples. The great thing about accepting Christ is that we accept His leadership and guidance. As we begin each day, it is important to invite God to take control. We must remember as Isaiah 43:2 reminds us—He is always with us. Through every situation, we can be confident because God is with us.

It does not matter if you are going to the doctor's office, the lawyer's office, the principal's office, the church office, or your office, the choice is yours; you can choose to go alone or to take God with you. Whatever you are facing, God will protect you and be with you. With each decision you need to make, God will help you and guide you. There are times when we feel like we are alone because we don't trust anyone with the situation we are facing, so we do not share. You can always talk to and trust God. He will direct you if you acknowledge His sovereignty in your life. We like to say God is sovereign because it is a popular statement. But if we really understand that it means supreme power and authority, then we also know that He has dominion over everything concerning us. Sometimes we are afraid, but we should still trust. Psalm 56:3 NIV says, "When I am afraid, I put my trust in you."

Proverbs 3:5–6 KJV says, "Trust in the Lord with all thine heart and lean not unto thine own understanding. In all of your ways acknowledge him, and he shall direct thy paths." Sometimes we think we understand so we lean to our own understanding. But if we condition our minds to hear what the spirit is saying, we will make the right decision. I encourage you today to allow Holy Spirit to lead and watch God work on your behalf.

UNCERTAINTY

Simon answered, "Master we've worked hard all night and haven't caught anything. But because you say so, I will let down the nets."

(LUKE 5:5 NIV)

There are times when life has a flow and all is good, in order, and according to plans. I am a planner and I like to plan as far into the future as possible in order to prepare. I plan my ministry by creating events and dates well in advance for the convenience of my participants. I make plans with my family and friends. I also plan my finances to be a good steward. It is a wonderful thing when well-made plans work out. But how many of you know that plans are subject to change and sometimes without notice? I must admit I was one who became frustrated with sudden changes at the hands of those who were not planners. After all, there is a difference in circumstances changing for a valid reason and lack of planning. I didn't like the uncertainty of how things would turn out if not well planned.

As I grew in my walk with Christ, I began to see His hand in my changes. Pay close attention because if He is truly the Lord of your life, you will too. I have had to make changes in my life that did not fit into "my" plans and seemed like moving backward to me. But God saw the road ahead and knew the change would be easier to make now than when I arrived at my destination.

Luke 5 tells the story of Jesus by the Lake of Gennesaret being pressed by the multitude. Jesus saw two boats that were empty because the fisherman were gone and washing their nets. Jesus chose one of the boats from which He would teach the people and asked Simon Peter to pull away from the shore a little and he taught the people from the boat. When Jesus had finished teaching, he told Simon Peter to go out where it is deeper and drop his net. Simon said, "We have been fishing all night and caught nothing, but okay I will do what you say."

Simon was a fisherman by trade, so he knew when the fish were most plentiful. In my mind I wonder if he was prepared to prove Jesus wrong about a catch at this point. And, he and his crew were probably tired from working all night and catching nothing. He may have had uncertainty about Jesus's request, but they did what Jesus asked them to do. In fact, after fishing all night and catching nothing, he may have had uncertainty about his future since this was his trade. But they dropped their nets, and the Bible says they caught so many fish that their nets broke and they had to call the other boat over to fill it also.

Do you have uncertainty today? Have you been working at something for a long time with seemingly no results? Does your future feel uncertain? Or, maybe you have well-organized plans in place and something has happened to make you feel uncertain about how it will all turn out.

Launch out into the deep today. Give your situation to God. Do what He tells you to do. You may be a pro like Simon, and think you know best. But let Simon be your example and make it personal and repeat after Simon: Master, I've been doing this a long time with no results, but just because you say so I will do this. Then do what He tells you.

Remember, God *must* be glorified in our lives. Perhaps He is waiting for you to allow Him to step into your boat so He can show you who He really is and the power of letting Him take control. From that day Simon Peter followed Jesus. Jesus told him he was now going to be a fisher of men. Are you heeding the call of God in your life?

My sister, at times of uncertainty, seek God and do whatever He tells you to do knowing He will be with you.

SALT AND LIGHT

You are the salt of the earth. But if the salt loses its saltiness, how can it be made salty again? It is no longer good for anything, except to be thrown out and trampled underfoot.

You are the light of the world. A town build on a hill cannot be hidden.

Neither do people light a lamp and put it under a bowl. Instead they put it on a stand, and it gives light to everyone in the house. In the same way, let your light shine before others, that they may see your good deeds and glorify your Father in heaven.

(MATTHEW 5:13–16 NIV)

I am a cook and I love trying new recipes. Recently I have been experimenting with a low-sodium diet. There is nothing worse than bland food, so salt is an important seasoning to help give food flavor. What I have found is that a pinch of salt brings out the flavor of all the other seasonings used in the recipe. I use the least amount of salt, but it has the biggest effect on the taste. Salt is so important that using old salt that has lost its flavor will not produce the results you are trying to achieve in your recipe. A well-seasoned meal will awaken your taste buds and help you to feel satisfied.

In Matthew 5 during the Sermon on the Mount, Jesus taught about salt and light. He asks the question, what good is salt if it has lost its flavor? The answer is that it is good for nothing, it has no value, and it has no effect. Flavor in food is altered or enhanced by adding particular ingredients. Jesus said we are the salt of the earth. We are the ingredient that enhances the world around us. Your presence in your home, on your job, and in your church should be the ingredient that enhances and creates a pleasant atmosphere. You should add value to those around you. People should feel better having you around. As Christians, we should not blend in with the world—we should have a positive effect bringing out the best in those around us just as salt brings out the best flavors in a meal.

We are also to shine bright like a light. We sometimes save that light until we leave home, but my sisters, the light needs to shine brightly at home first. How do we shine at home you may ask. By showing the same love to our family that we show at work or at church and by upholding the standard of holiness that God requires of us at home as well as at church. We should be the brightest light shining in our homes.

Light takes away darkness. Light is a natural agent that stimulates sight and makes things visible. When a light is turned on in a dark room, you suddenly see everything in that room, the good and bad. As our lights shine as women, we lead by example. We are living examples of God's love. As our lights shine, the first thing we should see is ourselves. The changes we need to make by removing any behavior that makes our light dim. That's when we see the things that we need to pray for. We see where we need to show more love. We also see where we need to take a stand.

Let your light shine so that people will see the power of God at work in your life. To be salt and light means to enhance our surroundings by illuminating the places God sends us. Be an influence, and make a difference. Remember people are watching how you live. Be salt and light in your world.

FLOURISH

Dear brothers and sisters, when troubles of any kind come your way, consider it an opportunity for great joy. For you know that when your faith is tested, your endurance has a chance to grow.

So let it grow, for when your endurance is fully developed, you will be perfect and complete, needing nothing.

(JAMES 1:2–4 NLT)

Sometimes bad things happen to good people. These bad things bring about trials or storms in our lives. Storms are a part of the seasons of life. Some days are sunny, and some days are dreary. But then there are days when it's cloudy and gloomy all day with severe thunderstorms.

How do you survive the storm? I remember when the children were young, a snowstorm meant not going to school, playing in the snow (for them), and having fun. A thunderstorm was a different story; sometimes we found ourselves laying around watching TV or reading in a quiet house. But many times, we were playing games and baking chocolate chip cookies (to eat as they came out of the oven) and just waiting for the storm to pass. That's so much different than how we behaved in storms when I was a child. We had to stop everything, turn everything off, and be quiet until the storm passed.

Just as there are different ways to survive storms naturally, so it is spiritually. Do you cover your head and peep out every now and then looking for that ray of sunshine to prove the storm has passed? Or, do you continue your normal activities waiting for the storm to pass over? Moving about normally is a sign that you are not afraid of the storm. Moving about with joy shows that you are trusting God as you go through the storm. We shouldn't just survive the storm—we should flourish in the storm. When you are flourishing, you are growing and developing. Ask yourself these questions: What is this storm trying to teach me? Am I repeating the same storm? As you know a storm is a test, and when we fail the test, we repeat it until we pass.

James tells us to count it all joy when we go through trials, because God is building endurance in us through the testing of our faith. Once endurance has been perfected, we become mature and complete. So, when we flourish, we develop rapidly and successfully—we thrive. To thrive is to prosper. As we go through storms with joy, we are developing character. Our goal should be to take on the characteristics of Jesus. If we want to reign with Him one day, we must learn to suffer as He did. We know He rose from the grave with all power and with the victory. We too can be victorious as we trust God to be with us through the storm. Sister, flourish, don't just survive!

Expectation

My soul, wait thou only upon God; for my expectation is
from him.

(Psalm 62:5 KJV)

Expectation is the act or state of expecting and anticipation in
expectation of what will happen. There are so many expectations
in life. We have standards by which we think people should behave,
and when they don't, we are disappointed.

One of the most difficult things to do is not react negatively
when we feel hurt or disappointed. We may be able to get over the
first offense, but what happens when it is a continuous cycle? The
test gets even harder when it's your child or your spouse. And what
about disappointment at church with the pastor or ministry leaders.
We have standards by which we judge those around us, and when
they are not met, it sometimes causes us to withdraw due to hurt and
disappointment.

I have definitely been disappointed many times in life. I found it
very easy to let go of people who constantly disappointed me until I
became mature in Christ. Once I stopped reacting in my feelings and

began to take those hurts to God, my reaction changed and so did my expectation. I began to realize people are incapable in their own strength of meeting my expectations. I learned that my expectation should be of God alone. I learned that God sometimes places people in our lives for a season. I also realized sometimes people are pruned because they are just toxic to our relationship. God knows what we need and when. I started to notice when an unmet expectation was a selfish desire and when it was a need. I was amazed to see how God met all my needs because He feels the deep longing in my soul.

We put so much pressure on our husbands, children, and friends when we are needy. We expect them to comfort us when we are sad, celebrate us when good things happen, listen to our problems, and more. But Psalm 62:5 KJV says, "my soul, wait thou only upon God; for my expectation is from him." Wow, those few words say a whole lot. What I found was releasing my feelings to God in prayer was way more powerful than expressing my disappointment to people. You see, people may become defensive or upset because they may not understand your feelings. God knows us intimately and He knows how to meet our innermost needs.

To wait is to stay right where you are and delay action until a particular time when something will happen and to be patient, to hold back. When we have expectation, we give hints to our husbands, we dump our problems on our friends, and we nag our children. But what if we spend time with God each day pouring our heart out to Him only? That's what I began to do, and I watched as God changed things around me and most of all changed *me*.

Trust God with your expectations and wait patiently for Him to act on your behalf.

Do You Believe

See, God has come to save me. I will trust in him and not be afraid. The Lord God is my strength and my song; he has given me victory.

(ISAIAH 12:2 NLT)

D o you believe that no matter how it looks right now, things can change? Do you believe in God's power to influence people to do what is right? Or, do you believe it is what it is and since it has not changed for so long, it will just be what it is? Have you heard people say that it is what it is?

Well, I choose to believe, and I have experienced God's power to influence people and to change situations. You see, sometimes we have said all we can say and done all we can do. Many times, our frustration with not seeing a change causes us to become depressed, discouraged, and maybe even bitter if we have been waiting for a long time. And what about situations when that change means you must still do the right thing by people who don't or have not done the right thing by you? Wow. That's a lot to carry.

The book of Isaiah is about God's judgment over Israel and other nations, but it is also about hope. I like chapter 12 verse 2 NLT that says, "God has come to save me, I will trust in him and not be afraid. The Lord God is my strength and my song; he has given me victory." That verse lets me know that even though my enemies come to overtake me, with God on my side, I *am* victorious. You see, chapter 12 of Isaiah is a song of praise for salvation. They are praising God for what they know is to come, when Jesus shall reign over the earth. We too should be praising Him and telling others that He will one day come back to reign over the earth.

To believe means to feel sure of the truth of something. As you pray over the situation you are facing, *believe* in God's power to change one of these: the situation, the person or circumstance, or *you* for the situation. I have come to realize that sometimes I need to change my attitude in a situation, my outlook on the situation, or the situation I'm in. How do I decide? I pray for wisdom and direction. As simple as that sounds it is not always easy, but it is effective.

I said, I *choose* to believe and have experienced God's power to change. There have been times when I felt hopeless but continued to move forward in what needed to be done realizing my service was unto God. I prayed for strength, I cried, and it hurt. There was nothing else I could do or say, so I stopped and just continued to do what I knew was pleasing to God. I am so grateful for strong spiritual women in my life to confide in when the load seemed too heavy because I knew they would pray. I am grateful for the Titus 2 women who took time to train me as a young woman in the way of holiness.

I believe, because as I let go, change began to take place. I stopped being angry about all the things that were wrong in my life and let God take control. I knew some people and situations would only change by His power. You see, only God can control the hearts and minds of people. We must trust Him to act on our behalf because He knows what we need. There's a song that simply says, only believe, all things are possible if you only believe.

A LITTLE DEEPER

Cast all your anxiety on him because he cares for you.

(1 PETER 5:7 NIV)

As Christians, we have developed a relationship with God through some sort of experience that introduced us to His power and saving grace. In the beginning we are excited as we begin this new journey. As time goes on, we may come to a place where we are maintaining by attending church regularly on Sunday, possibly a bible study now and then, and we may or may not become involved in other ministry. Some of us remain on the surface and some go a little deeper.

Daily life is very demanding. As people are living much longer, not only are parents raising their own children, but many times they are assisting aging parents either in their own homes, their parents' home, or a nursing home. Single parents are tasked with the responsibilities of two parents just to keep the household in order. We genuinely struggle with the thought of adding more of anything to our lives beyond home and career. We fit God in where we can.

The call to go a little deeper is a call to take you to a deeper level spiritually. 1 Peter 5:7 NIV tells us to cast our anxiety on God because

He cares. God knows the responsibility we carry and the burdens we bear daily. He is concerned and just waiting for us to come to Him. In Matthew 11:28 NIV, Jesus said, "Come to me all who are weary and burdened and I will give you rest." Resting in Jesus happens at a deeper level where you cannot even explain the peace you feel in the storm. You feel confident that everything will work out. You find strength for the daily tasks and demands. You find wisdom to make the right decisions. You find love to extend to those around you. And you find joy in sorrow and pain. But this does not just happen; we must do our part to deepen the relationship. He wants to carry our burdens if we will let Him. Any relationship must be nurtured if we are to reach a level of intimacy and closeness. And our relationship with Jesus is no different.

But how do we get there? Philippians 4:6–7 NIV tells us, "Do not be anxious about anything, but in every situation, by prayer and petition, with thanksgiving, present your requests to God. And the peace of God, which transcends all understanding, will guard your hearts and your minds in Christ Jesus." That's the first step—tell God all about it. Tell Him everything that hinders your time with Him, and ask Him to show you how to make room for Him in your life. Spend time in prayer. Study the Bible. Find opportunities to do good to others. Fellowship with other believers.

Maybe the busyness in your life has caused you to lose focus on your spirituality. Why not begin today to go a little deeper? Going deeper means setting aside time to focus on God through praying and reading His word. As you begin to take one step at a time, you will soon discover your burdens feel lighter because you are allowing God to carry them for you. As you learn His word and talk to Him in prayer, you will be amazed how much more you are drawn to Him.

Come on sister, let's go a little deeper in our walk with God.

Look Up

We do this by keeping our eyes on Jesus, the champion who initiates and perfects our faith. Because of the joy awaiting him, he endured the cross, disregarding its shame. Now he is seated in the place of honor beside God's throne.

(Hebrews 12:2 NLT)

A hung down head is a sign of feeling defeated. We also bow our heads when we are sad or discouraged. Sometimes the very load of life seems too much and can feel like we are carrying weights. Even the strongest Christians struggle and feel defeated at times. We wonder if we are moving in the right direction in life and if we are really doing what God has called us to do.

One Sunday morning, I was reading my devotional for the day when I received a text from a dear friend that said, "look up and see God, your help is on the way." That was it, short and to the point. I responded assuming she knew my husband was soon to have open-heart surgery. She had no clue, but just as so many others had done during this time, she was obeying God and saying what He told her to say.

What a timely text. God was letting me know He was sending me everything I need for the days and weeks to come. I received the message by faith not knowing what was ahead of me. Hebrews is the book of the Bible about faith. It teaches us about sacrifice, maturity, faith, and endurance. Hebrews 12:2 tells us to look unto Jesus, the champion who initiates and perfects our faith. Jesus looked beyond what He was facing to the joy that would come later. As Christians we must remember we will have struggles, but we must keep our eyes on Jesus and not our situation or circumstances.

Looking up means we are keeping our eyes on Jesus and trusting by faith that He will see us through. There are people who have faced unbelievable obstacles and been victorious because they kept looking up. Sometimes we look down in defeat or look straight ahead into our situation. But when we look to heaven, it reminds us that Jesus is there looking over us and guiding our steps.

David Jeremiah said when people see courage, they are drawn to it. Overcoming your adversity with courage is a testimony to the grace and mercy of God. As people see you trust God, they will have hope in their own situations. We are living testimonies to the power, mercy, and grace of God.

There is a song that says "look up and see God, your help is on the way." As I talked to God about my needs, He sent people all around us to meet those needs. Romans 8:28 NKJV reminds us that all things work together for good to those who love God, to those who are the called according to His purpose.

My sister, I know life can be difficult and sometimes the things we go through don't make sense or seem fair. Remember, if we are to reign with Christ, we must also suffer as He did. Just look up and keep your eyes on Jesus and He will see you through.

The Healing Power of Jesus

Just then a woman who had been subject to bleeding for twelve years came up behind him and touched the edge of his cloak. She said to herself, "If I only touch his cloak, I will be healed."

Jesus turned and saw her. "Take heart, daughter," he said, "your faith has healed you." And the woman was healed at that moment.

(Matthew 9:20–22 NIV)

T he Bible is filled with stories about healing. As Jesus traveled about, he encountered many that were sick and afflicted. There were times when Jesus healed them, but there were other times when He let the person know it was their own faith that made them well. We find this in the story of the ten lepers and blind beggar in Luke and the centurion in Matthew. The woman in Matthew 9 had suffered for twelve years but was certain that if she could just touch Jesus, she would be healed. She wasn't trying to meet him or have a face-to-face encounter; she just wanted to get close enough to touch His cloak.

Faith and healing go hand in hand. We must first believe without doubting that Jesus is able to heal us and accept the healing however

He sends it. When Jesus heals, doctors cannot explain it—they just know what they see. I have witnessed how God allows us to go through the process, so we have written proof of what He does. The process also strengthens us as the scripture tells us in 1 Peter 5:10 NIV: after you have suffered a little while, the God of all grace will Himself restore you and make you strong, firm, and steadfast. Don't resist the process.

Have you experienced the healing power of Jesus? I have in many ways. Sometimes we don't recognize that a situation we survived was God's healing power over us. Surviving an abusive relationship requires healing to be made whole again. You can be healed from church hurt, physical or mental illness, depression, insecurity, low self-esteem, and much more. I have experienced the healing power of Jesus in so many ways. I have also witnessed healing in others, some very close to me.

It doesn't matter how long you have been sick; Jesus is able to heal you. The woman in the scripture today had been sick for twelve years. She pressed through the crowd strongly believing even if she just touched the hem of His robe and He didn't even lay hands on her or see her, she would be healed. She did get close enough to touch His garment, and the amazing thing is that He stopped and asked, "Who touched Me?" My sister, believe in His power to heal you. Jesus is not walking among us as in this woman's time, but you can touch Him through prayer and worship. And believe me, He will know His daughter is reaching out for Him and will stop by your situation.

Just know today that you are special to Jesus, and if you cry out to Him, He will hear you. Yes, the multitudes are always pressing to get to Him. There are constant requests being made for healing, deliverance, strength, and much more. But while honoring those requests, He loves you enough to stop and hear your cry. My sister, reach out and touch Him today.

The man in John 5 KJV at the pool of Bethesda had been sick for thirty-eight years. The scripture says in verse 4, "For an angel went down at a certain season into the pool and troubled the water: and whosoever then first after the troubling of the water stepped in was made whole of whatever disease he had." When Jesus saw the man, He knew he had been in that condition a long time and asked him if he wanted to be made well. The man said he had no one to put him into the pool and every time he tried to get there, someone went ahead of him. Jesus said, "Rise, take up thy bed and walk."

Jesus could have called the disciples to put the man into the pool, but instead He healed him right where he was. How comforting to know that Jesus will meet us and heal us right where we are. Do you have a place where you meet Jesus daily? He can heal you there. Do you have a place where you worship daily? He can heal you there.

What are you struggling with today? Do you want to be made whole? Cry out to Jesus right where you are, and ask Him to heal you and make you whole.

Strength in the Fire

When thou passest through the waters, I will be with thee; and
through the rivers, they shall not overflow thee: when thou
walkest through the fire, thou shalt not be burned: neither
shall the flame kindle upon thee.

(Isaiah 43:2 KJV)

F ire is beautiful to watch. I prefer a wood-burning fireplace because
the flames are more intense and their beauty relaxes me. I remember poking the fire trying to keep it burning so it would last as long
as possible. Fire is beautiful but can also be very destructive. People
trapped in a building on fire sometimes don't survive. It is almost
impossible to be in a raging fire without being burned or consumed.
There are times when people are rescued from fires, but seldom without some effect of the experience.

Fires are extinguished by saturation with a substance that destroys
the flame. Once the flame is extinguished, the danger is not over
because we need to watch for embers. Those tiny embers can catch
onto something and cause another fire to begin. It is also interesting
that embers also signify the end of a fire as they glow brightly.

In Isaiah 42, God is disappointed with the spiritual failure of His chosen people, Israel. In chapter 43 God says despite His disappointment, He will restore them and bring them out of captivity. The Bible says when we go through deep waters, God will be with us. When we go through rivers of difficulty, we will not drown. And when we walk through the fire, we will not be burned. The flame will not even kindle upon us.

The *Oxford Dictionary*'s definition of kindle is to light or set on fire. Another definition is to arouse or inspire an emotion or feeling. The scripture is saying when we go through the fire, He will be with us and we will not be set on fire by the situation. If we rest in Him, the situation will not even arouse our emotions. Wow, that's so powerful. Imagine the worst trial you have ever experienced—that's your fire. Now imagine coming out not looking like what you have been through because God did not allow the fire to burn you; in fact the flame didn't even kindle upon you.

I went through a very trying situation recently. I heard Holy Spirit speaking quietly to me to do as much as I could to be quiet and not deal with the situation emotionally. I would rise very early in the morning to begin my day with quiet time by spending time in prayer and meditation. I also did not allow the opinions of others to determine the outcome of the situation. We are not always able to ignore people's chatter, but we must learn to not allow it to penetrate our spirit and move us from our position.

Are you going through a difficult situation right now? Believe me when I say God's word is true when it says He will be with you. Quiet your mind and don't let the chatter around you determine what you will choose to believe. Remember to hold on to the word of God and to whatever He speaks to your spirit. I remember during my quiet time I would repeatedly hear Philippians 4:19 KJV: "but my God shall supply all your need according to his riches in glory by Christ Jesus" (Philippians 4:19 KJV). And He certainly did. There was nothing I needed that God did not supply. Trust God today and you will find strength in the fire!

INTEGRITY

Righteousness guards the person of integrity, but wickedness
overthrows the sinner.

(PROVERBS 13:6 NIV)

In Proverbs 22:1 KJV the Bible says a good name is rather to be
chosen than great riches. Proverbs is known as a book of wisdom
and often compares the life of a wicked man as opposed to the life
of a righteous man. I would guess this subject was addressed because
sometimes people think more about riches than reputation. Your reputation comes from beliefs or opinions people form based on your
behavior. We work very hard to achieve riches, but do we work just as
hard to have a good reputation? People who have a good reputation are
considered trustworthy and kind. Often a person with a good name is
said to be a man or woman of integrity. A good name is rather to be
chosen than great riches, and loving favor rather than silver and gold
(Proverbs 22:1 KJV).

Integrity is being honest and having strong moral principles.
Morals are the principles of right and wrong and good and bad behavior. Integrity is not only doing right when people are watching but

doing the right thing when no one is watching or knows that you chose to be honest. One of the most difficult things for some people, even Christians, is to stand for what's right even when you have to stand alone. A person with integrity does not hang out in the gray area which represents a little bit of black (wrong) and a little bit of white (right). A person with integrity stands for what is right, period.

Philippians 4:8 KJV encourages us to think on things that are true, honest, just, pure, lovely, and of good report. Romans 12:2 KJV tells us to not conform to the world but to be transformed by the renewing of our minds. These scriptures are so important in our walk as Christians. Applying God's word gives us the strength to walk in integrity and moral excellence.

As disciples of Christ, we need not walk in fear. Fear may cause us to behave in a way that is dishonest. 2 Timothy 1:7 KJV lets us know that God has not given us a spirit of fear, but of power, love, and a sound mind. We must always remember, as we walk in integrity, we are honoring God. You may never know who is watching you and patterning their life after yours, so it pays to always do what is right.

Take a moment to reflect on your life. Are you a person of integrity? Do you stand for what's right regardless of the consequences? What type of fruit have you produced? I took one month with thirty-one days and read one chapter of Proverbs each day. Proverbs was written as an instruction on attaining wisdom and living a prudent life. The book ends with the characteristics of a virtuous woman in chapter 31. This is a familiar chapter to many of us as women. Take time to reflect and identify areas in your life where you can grow in wisdom and integrity.

Loving God More

And at midnight Paul and Silas prayed, and sang praises unto God: and the prisoners heard them.

And suddenly there was a great earthquake, so that the foundations of the prison were shaken: and immediately all the doors were opened, and every one's bands were loosed.

(Acts 16:25–26 KJV)

There are different seasons in life. We may be in a summer season where all is well and the sun is shining bright in our hearts even on rainy days. We may find ourselves in and out of spring and fall with a problem here and there, but we can handle it. Then there are times when winter seems to suddenly appear. Sometimes there is no warning. It's like the big snowstorm no one is expecting right before spring or at the end of fall. Oh, how pretty. The glistening snow sparkles, and we take time to enjoy all that it brings. A snowstorm is pretty, but if winter is not your favorite season (like me), you want it to end *now*.

The same can be true in our spiritual walk. Things are going well. We are working diligently in our ministry. Our prayers are being answered. Family and work are going well. Then winter strikes. How do you react in your winter season? Do you settle in and wait for it to pass? Do you give in to feelings of depression and oppression? Or, do you press forward knowing that God is still there and in control?

In Acts chapter 16, Paul is on his second missionary journey. Paul, Silas, and Timothy were traveling to different cities preaching and teaching, and people were accepting the good news of the gospel. They were also instructing the believers who were becoming strong in their faith. Along with all the good, they also encountered a demon-possessed girl who was a fortune-teller. After many days of the demon following and annoying them, Paul cast out the demon. The masters of the girl became angry because she was very profitable for them, and they took Paul and Silas before the authorities. Paul and Silas were stripped, beaten, and thrown in jail.

You may not suffer the physical persecution Paul and Silas faced because of your faith, but you may wonder why you are suffering, because you too try to do good and live a Godly life. James 1:2–4 KJV tells us to count it as joy when we face various trials because the trying of our faith worketh patience.

Paul and Silas were put in stocks and thrown into prison. The Bible tells us around midnight they were praying and singing. They were having praise and worship right there in prison, even while their bodies were sore from the beating and they were bound. There were so many negative thoughts they could have been thinking. They could even have blamed God and given up on their faith. But Paul and Silas chose to love God more than their situation. They chose to pray and sing praises to God.

What about you? How do you react when trouble comes? Do you pout and cry? Maybe throw a tantrum or shut down and allow the weight of the situation to change your character? Or do you choose to trust God and love Him more than your situation and your pain? Loving God more means running *to* Him and not *away* from Him. It means trusting His wisdom and guidance. It means knowing He has a plan for you even during your winter season. No, you don't love the situation, but you can love God through the situation by continuing to praise and worship Him. You can choose to stay focused and on course during the storm.

According to therecord.com, a very bad winter may actually be good agriculturally as heavy snowstorms soak the ground with water to help feed crops as farmers begin to plant in early spring. The plants have water to draw from until the spring rain begins. The extreme cold kills harmful bugs and bacteria.

I found that very interesting because I know God has definitely used my winter seasons to prepare me for harvest. During winter we typically spend more time inside working on projects such as clearing clutter, throwing out junk, and organizing our lives. Wow. What if we changed our perspective of our spiritual winter and time of isolation and used it to soak up all we can to water those new seeds God wants to plant in our lives and ministry? What if we were to allow the extreme cold of winter to kill harmful spiritual bugs and bacteria that threaten to kill our harvest? What if we clear the clutter and throw out the junk in our minds and allow God's spirit to flow freely through us?

To begin the process of changing our perspective, let's vow today to love God more than our hurts and pain. Let's love God through our sickness. Let's love God more than our disappointment. How? By worshipping, praising, and honoring Him through our bad times just as we do in good times. Remember how at midnight Paul and Silas prayed and sang praises to God until there was an earthquake that caused the very foundation to shake. Sister, praise Him until the shackles of your life are loosed, until doors are opened, and until everyone around you knows that God is real. You see, the scripture does not say that the bands were loosed from just Paul and Silas—it says everyone's band was loosed. Remember, your attitude and love for God also affect those around you. Sister, choose to love God more!